SPANISH
for children

Catherine Bruzzone

Illustrations
Clare Beaton

PASSPORT BOOKS
a division of *NTC Publishing Group*
Lincolnwood, Illinois USA

Also available:
German for Children
Italian for Children
French for Children
Inglés para niños
Each title in this series is a complete home learning course
with cassettes and a colorful children's Activity Book.

**PRODUCED FOR PASSPORT BOOKS
BY B SMALL PUBLISHING**

Spanish edition
Rosa María Martín

Editor
Catherine Bruzzone

Design and Art Direction
Lone Morton

Typesetting
Lone Morton and Olivia Norton

Recordings
Gerald Ramshaw, Max II

Music
David Stoll

Lyrics
Rosa María Martín and David Stoll

Presenter
Rosa María Martín

Singers
Peter Ryan and Isabelle Wilmet

With special thanks to Rosa María Martín and her family, the children
of the village of Belchite, Spain, and Joaquín Barriga and the
Centro Cívico Delicias, Zaragoza, Spain.

1997 Printing

Published by Passport Books, a division of NTC Publishing Group.
©1993 by NTC Publishing Group, 4255 West Touhy Avenue, Lincolnwood (Chicago), Illinois 60646-1975 U.S.A.
All rights reserved. No part of this book may be reproduced, stored in a retrieval system, or transmitted in
any form or by any means, electronic, mechanical, photocopying, recording or otherwise, without the prior
permission of NTC Publishing Group.
Printed in Hong Kong

7 8 9 0 WKT 9 8 7 6

Contents

Learning Spanish

Here are 10 simple suggestions to make learning Spanish with Passport's *Spanish for Children* much more fun:

 Learn with someone else if you can: perhaps a friend, your mom or dad, sister or brother. This course is full of games, so it's nice to have someone to play them with.

 Start with the cassette. Rosa will tell you what to do and when to use the book. Just remember to read Fun Facts and Supergato and fill in the Checklist.

 Listen for a short while, then go and do something else. But don't give up! When you listen again, you'll be amazed how much you remember.

 Rewind and fast-forward the cassette, and go over any section as often as you like.

 Say everything out loud – don't keep it to yourself. You could practice while you're taking a bath or out on your bike.

 Don't worry if you make mistakes. That's just part of learning a language.

 Sometimes an English word can help you remember the Spanish: "chocolate" and **chocolate**, "family" and **familia**, for example.

 Start a Spanish scrapbook and put in everything you can discover about Mexico, Spain – and all the other countries where Spanish is spoken. There are at least 22 of them.

 If you're learning with a friend, give each other Spanish names. There are some suggestions for names below.

 Enjoy yourself! It's a lot of fun speaking another language . . . and one day it might be very useful too.

Spanish names

Boys		*Girls*	
Carlos	José	Ana	Elena
Enrique	Juan	Beatriz	Elisa
Felipe	Luis	Carmen	Margarita
Fernando	Manuel	Conchita	Marta

1 ¡Yo!

This is Rosa.
You'll hear her voice
on the tape.
She's going to help you
learn Spanish.

Right from the start, you're going to learn:

- to say "hello"
- how to answer when someone asks you your name
- the numbers from 1 to 10
- how to answer when someone asks you how old you are.

Before you go on, listen to the tape.
Rosa will tell you what to do.
First, she's saying hello.
The words for the two songs you will hear are on page 69.

Naming names

Put an ✘ in the box when you hear the name.

☐	☐	☐	☐
José	**Teresa**	**Carlos**	**Ana**

Put your name here!

¡hola!
hello, hi

¿cómo te llamas?
what's your name?

me llamo _____
my name is

Fun Facts

Altogether, over 300 million people in the world speak Spanish as their first language. There are at least twenty-five countries where Spanish is spoken: Spain, Mexico, and Colombia are three. Can you discover any more?

Do you know the Spanish name for Spain? It is **España**, and comes from the name given to it by the Romans that means "Land of the Rabbits." Colombia, in South America, is named after **Cristóbal Colón**, Christopher Columbus, the great explorer.

Many Spanish names mean interesting things if you translate them into English. For girls, **Milagros** means "miracles," **Socorro** means "help," **Dolores** means "pains." For boys, **Domingo** is "Sunday," and **Julio** is "July."

¡Vamos a contar juntos!

Listen to the tape.
Count these things with Rosa, and write the number in the box.

How old am I?

Listen to the tape. Match up the names with the ages.
The first one has been done for you.

Marta

Mari Carmen

Coco

9   8   4   5   7   10

Chita

Juan

Luis

¿cuántos años tienes?

how old are you?

Put your age here!

tengo _____ años

I'm _____ (years old)

¡Hola!

8

Draw a picture of yourself here. Why not add a speech bubble with **¡Hola!** (hello!)?

¡Yo! Me!

Me llamo _____ .

Tengo ___ años.

¿qué tal?
how are things?

bien, gracias
fine, thanks

Checklist

Let's go over what you have learned in this unit. When you are sure you know what these mean, put a ✔ in the box.

☐ **uno** **dos** **tres** **cuatro** **cinco** **seis** **siete** **ocho** **nueve** **diez**

☐ **¡hola!**

☐ **me llamo** _____

☐ **¿cómo te llamas?**

☐ **tengo _____ años**

☐ **¿cuántos años tienes?**

☐ **¿qué tal? bien, gracias**

> Try and say these out loud. If you have any trouble with them, why not listen to the tape again?

¡Super gato!

¡Hola! Me llamo Supergato.

Uno, dos, tres, cuatro.

¡Hola! Me llamo Monstruorata!

2 María y Javier

In this unit, you're going to learn:

- to say whether you like something or not
- to say "yes" and "no," and
- the names of some popular – and unpopular – things!

What are they saying?

First listen to the tape.
Now cut out the sentences below and paste them into the right bubbles. Now can you fill in the blanks?

Javier

María

Tengo _____ **años**	**Me llamo** _____
¡Hola!	**Tengo** _____ **años** **¡Hola!**
	Me llamo _____

11

I like . . .

Listen to the tape. Draw a line between **Sí** and the things you like and **No** and the things you don't.

Sí  No

The words for the song are on page 69.

me gusta/me gustan . . .	
I like . . .	
¿te gusta?/¿te gustan?	
do you like?	
sí yes	**no** no

Fun Facts

Did you know that chocolate comes from the cacao bean? A Spanish explorer, Hernan Cortez first discovered this bean in Mexico and took it to Europe. The cocoa bean was even used as a coin by the Maya Indians in Mexico.

Lunch is eaten very late in Spain, around 2 o'clock, so snacks in the bar before lunch are very popular. You can have a drink and a **tapa**, or a **banderilla**, mouth-watering small snacks made with things like olives, shellfish, red peppers, and anchovies.

In Spain a fruit juice is called **zumo**, but in Latin America it is also called **jugo**.

tapas

In Mexico, if you want a healthy and refreshing drink, try a **licuado**, a fresh fruit milk shake. You can buy a similar kind of drink in Spain, called a **batido**. A **batido de fresa** is a strawberry milk shake. Yum yum!

¿Sí o no?

Listen to the tape.
María and Javier's shopping trip.
If María or Javier say they like something, check the box next to the right picture below. Then cut those pictures out and paste them in the basket on page 15.

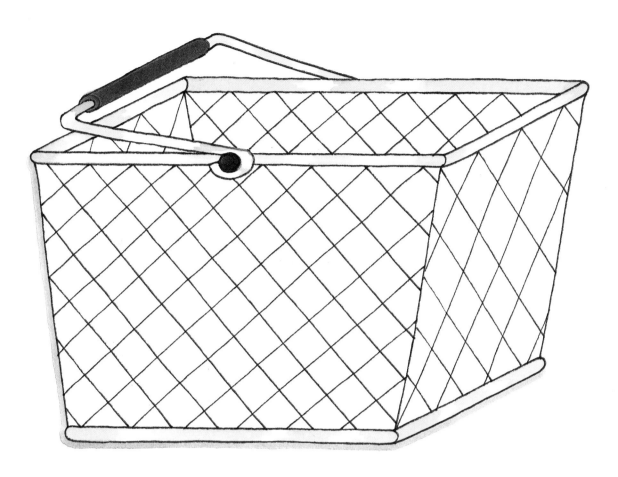

la Coca-Cola Coca-Cola
la gaseosa lemonade
el chocolate chocolate
el gato cat
el helado ice cream
la fresa strawberry
la pizza pizza
la bruja witch
la araña spider
el monstruo monster

Checklist

Let's go over what you have learned in this unit. When you are sure you know what these mean, put a ✔ in the box.

☐ **me gusta/me gustan**

☐ **¿te gusta?/¿te gustan?**

☐ **sí**

☐ **no**

☐ **el chocolate**
la Coca-Cola
el helado
la gaseosa
la pizza

el gato
la araña
el monstruo
la fresa
la bruja

Try and say these out loud. If you have any trouble with them, why not listen to the tape again?

¡Super gato!

Me gusta el chocolate, el helado y la gaseosa.

BANCO

A mí me gusta el oro.

banco = bank
el oro = gold

¡Ay, una araña!

3 En el colegio

In this unit, you're going to learn:

- how to ask where something is
- how to say "goodbye" and "thank you"
- and some words about school.

Deal a number

This is a simple card game to practice
the numbers from 1 to 10.
You need a deck of cards and a die – and a partner.
You need only the 1 to 10 of hearts and the 1 to 10 of spades.
The ace counts as 1. Shuffle the hearts and deal out five cards each.
Shuffle the spades and lay them around in a clock shape, face down.
Decide who goes first.

1 *Player 1*: you throw the die and call out the number in Spanish.
2 Move around the clock face that number of cards, counting out
   loud in Spanish as you go. Use the die as a counter.
3 When you land, turn over the card and say the number it shows,
   out loud in Spanish.
4 If the number matches a card in your hand, pick it up and lay
   down the pair. If not, turn it face down again.
5 *Player 2*: now you throw the die, call out the number, and move
   on around the clock just like Player 1.
6 The first player with all the pairs wins.

Now listen to the tape. First you will hear a song about
school. The words are at the back of the book on page 70.

Pedro's first day

Listen to the tape and point to the places and things around the picture. As you point say, **"allí"** (there).

el colegio the school

la clase

el lavabo

la puerta

el servicio

el patio

los amigos

la profesora

¿dónde está?
where is?
¿dónde están?
where are?
allí there

Fun Facts

In Spain, children start elementary school, called **escuela** or **colegio**, when they are six.

In Mexico and Colombia the school day starts very early, often at seven or eight o'clock in the morning; but it finishes at one o'clock and the children are free for the rest of the day!

School holidays, **las vacaciones**, are different in different parts of the Spanish-speaking world. For example in Spain and Mexico, the longest holiday is in June, July and August. But in Argentina it is over Christmas, **Navidad**. But of course, Christmas is the hottest time of the year in Argentina. Do you know why?

Guess the card

Play this game with a friend.
Make 9 cards: trace or copy the pictures around the edge of the playground scene on pages 18 and 19. Shuffle them and lay them out face down.

1 *Player 1:* will ask where something is. Use, "**¿dónde está?**" or "**¿dónde están?**"
2 *Player 2:* points to a card and says, "**allí.**"
3 If the guess is right, *Player 2* wins a point.
4 The first player with 10 points wins.
   (Shuffle the cards between each try.)

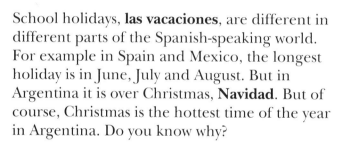

Now go on to the activity on page 21 before you go back to the tape.

Hidden pictures

There are three things hidden in this picture.
Can you find them? These questions will give you a clue.

¿Dónde está el chocolate?
¿Dónde está el gato?
¿Dónde están los amigos?

Then go back to the tape.

gracias	thank you
adiós	goodbye

Checklist

Let's go over what you have learned in this unit. When you are sure you know what these mean, put a ✔ in the box.

- ☐ **¿dónde está?**
- ☐ **¿dónde están?**
- ☐ **allí**
- ☐ **gracias**
- ☐ **adiós**

Try and say these out loud. If you have any trouble with them, why not listen to the tape again?

- ☐ **el colegio**   **la puerta**
  la profesora   **el patio**
  los amigos   **el servicio**
  la clase   **el lavabo**

¡Super gato!

Me llamo Inspector Gordo.

inspector = inspector
gordo = big, fat

BANCO

¡Oh no!, ¡la puerta!
¿Dónde está el oro?

Mon-struorata es el ladrón??

el ladrón = the thief

¿Dónde está Supergato?

Allí.

22

4 Mi familia

In this unit, you're going to learn:

- the names for "mom," "dad," "sister," and "brother"
- how you would be introduced to someone's family
- how to introduce your own family
- how to say how many brothers and sisters you have.

But first, listen to the tape and try the quiz. Then do the word puzzle below.

Puzzle

See if you can find these words hidden in the square. They're the same as the ones in the quiz, so you should know what they mean.

T	C	S	F	D	I	E	Z	K	S
I	U	S	C	W	O	L	B	H	O
S	A	T	E	A	E	V	D	O	S
N	T	A	R	T	O	I	M	L	U
S	R	P	G	R	A	C	I	A	S
G	O	R	N	E	U	R	G	J	T
O	D	A	U	S	T	O	N	S	Í
S	F	R	C	E	O	P	A	E	H
R	A	D	I	Ó	S	L	H	N	E
C	Q	N	H	L	N	O	M	O	N

TRES
CUATRO
ADIÓS
DOS
SÍ
GRACIAS
HOLA
DIEZ

La familia Bumerán

Listen to the tape. You'll be meeting this kangaroo family.

mi hermana
Margarita

Mamá

Papá

Rosita   mi hermano Pepito   mi hermana Elisa

The words for the song are on page 70.

ésta es/éste es   here is
la familia   family
papá   dad
mamá   mom
mi hermana   my sister
mi hermano   my brother

Fun Facts

In Spanish-speaking countries, people have two last names, **apellidos**, one from their father and the other from their mother. For example, if your father is named **Fernando García Martínez**, and your mother is named **Carmen Yuste Pérez**, *your* last name is **García Yuste**.

In Mexico, **el día de los muertos**, the Day of the Dead, on November 2nd is a special day when Mexicans remember members of their family who have died. But it is not a sad occasion. The children receive toys and candy in the shape of skulls, **calaveras**, or skeletons, **esqueletos**, made of chocolate, sugar, or marzipan.

In Spain, grandparents often live together with their children and grandchildren. The grandparents, **los abuelos**, sometimes look after their grandchildren, **los nietos**, while their parents, **los padres**, go out to work.

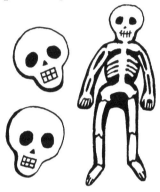

tengo ____ hermanos	I've got ____ brothers
tengo ____ hermanas	I've got ____ sisters
no tengo hermanos	I don't have any brothers
no tengo hermanas	I don't have any sisters

Mi familia

Draw a picture of your own family.
Copy the labels below, so you can describe your picture in Spanish. Then try the game on page 27.

| mi hermana | mi hermano | Mamá | Papá |

tengo ___ hermanas

tengo ___ hermanos

no tengo hermanos

no tengo hermanas

You may also need:
my grandma, **mi abuelita**, and my grandpa, **mi abuelito**

Ésta es mi familia

This is an "introducing game" for 2 players.
You need a die and two markers (buttons will do fine).
Decide who goes first.

 mamá

 papá

1 *Player 1:* throw the die and move that number of spaces – count in Spanish as you go!

 mi hermana

2 When you land, introduce the person who appears on that square to *Player 2*. Say, **"éste es . . . "** or **"ésta es . . . "**

mi hermano

3 *Player 2:* you reply, **"hola,"** and then it's your turn.
4 The first player to reach the ice cream wins.

27

Checklist

Let's go over what you have learned in this unit. When you are sure you know what these mean, put a ✔ in the box.

- [ ] **éste/ésta es**

- [ ] **mamá   papá**

- [ ] **mi hermano**
  mi hermana

- [ ] **tengo _____ hermanos**

- [ ] **tengo _____ hermanas**

- [ ] **no tengo hermanos**

- [ ] **no tengo hermanas**

Try and say these out loud. If you have any trouble with them, why not listen to the tape again?

¡Super

La familia de Monstruorata.

¡Aquí está papá!

gato!

Tengo cinco sacos de oro.

sacos = sacks
de oro = of gold

¡Gracias, papá!

28

5 La casa

In this unit, you're going to learn:

- another answer to "where is?" **(¿dónde está?)**
- how to ask "what's that?" – very useful if you don't know the name of something in Spanish!
- and how to give the answer
- to understand the word for "please"
- the names for rooms and furniture in the home.

Start with this game.
Listen to the tape before you read ahead.

Which hand?

You've probably played this game before. Now play it in Spanish!
You'll need a partner. You're going to guess which
hand your partner's holding something in.
Find a pebble, **una piedra.**

1 Now one of you will hold the pebble
   behind your back and ask your partner:
   "¿Dónde está la piedra?"
2 Your partner must touch one of your
   arms and say **"allí"** (there).
3 If it's right, he or she wins one point.
4 Then change places.
5 The first to get 10 points wins.

La casa de una bruja

Listen to the tape. You'll find out whose house this is.

el cuarto de baño

un lavabo

un frigorífico

la puerta

una mesa

la cocina

¿qué es esto? what's this?
es it's
está aquí it's here
por favor please

el dormitorio

una cama

una silla

el salón

una tele

¿Qué es esto?

You'll need a partner to play this game.
First cut out some small pieces of paper, this size:
and cover the pictures in the maze below.

1 *Player 1:* call out a number from 1 to 6 in Spanish.
2 *Player 2:* start from that number and find the way to the picture.
3 Uncover it and ask, "**¿qué es esto?**"
4 *Player 1:* Give the answer, "**es un . . .**" or "**es una . . .**"
5 Then it's *Player 2's* turn to call a number.

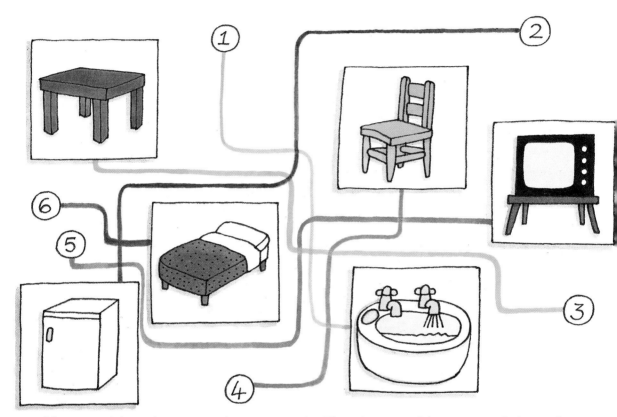

You could make new picture cards like these with some of the other words you know and play the game again.

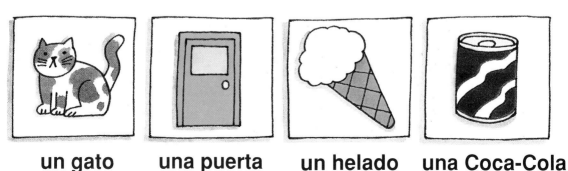

un gato　　**una puerta**　　**un helado**　　**una Coca-Cola**

Fun Facts

Houses and apartments in Spanish-speaking countries usually have **patios** or balconies with lots of plants and brightly colored flowers.

The windows have blinds, **persianas**, that keep out the very bright sunlight and allow you to take a **siesta**, an afternoon nap, after a good meal. In the hottest months, when it's too hot to go out in the middle of the day, children also take a **siesta**, but they don't like it very much!

In Spain, a bedroom is a **dormitorio**, but in Mexico it is called a **recámara**.

Many houses have iron grills at their windows, called **rejas** in Spain. They are decorative and have very beautiful designs.

Listen to the song on tape. You can join in with the words, which are on page 71 at the back of the book.

Checklist

Let's go over what you have learned in this unit. When you are sure you know what these mean, put a ✔ in the box.

☐ **¿qué es esto?**

☐ **es un/una . . .**

☐ **está aquí**

☐ **por favor**

Try and say these out loud. If you have any trouble with them, why not listen to the tape again?

☐ **la casa**
la cocina
el cuarto de baño
el salón
el dormitorio

una mesa
un frigorífico
una silla
una tele
una cama

6 De viaje

In this unit, you're going to learn:

• to say what you like doing
• to say what you don't like doing
• to count up to 20.

Spot the differences

First, there are 5 differences between these two pictures.
Can you spot them? The answers are under Picture 1.
Next, can you name 8 things in Picture 1,
out loud in Spanish?
You'll hear the answers on tape.

Label on bottle; picture; cakes on plate;
dials on TV; pattern on tablecloth.

En coche

Listen to the tape.
What does the Morales family like to do in the car?

The words for the song are at the back of your book on page 71.

¿qué te gusta hacer? what do you like to do?
me gusta leer I like to read
me gusta escuchar la radio I like to listen to the radio
me gusta comer I like to eat
me gusta cantar I like to sing
no me gusta comer I don't like to eat
no me gusta cantar I don't like to sing

Speeding and traffic jams

This is a game like *Chutes and Ladders* – you speed up the empty freeways and crawl back down into the traffic jams! You'll need a partner, two markers (buttons will do), and a die.
The first to get to the country in the last square wins.
If you land on any of these pictures, you must say, in Spanish:

 I like to listen to the radio

 I don't like to listen to the radio

 I like to eat

 I like to sing

 I like to read

 I don't like to read

 I don't like to eat

 I don't like to sing

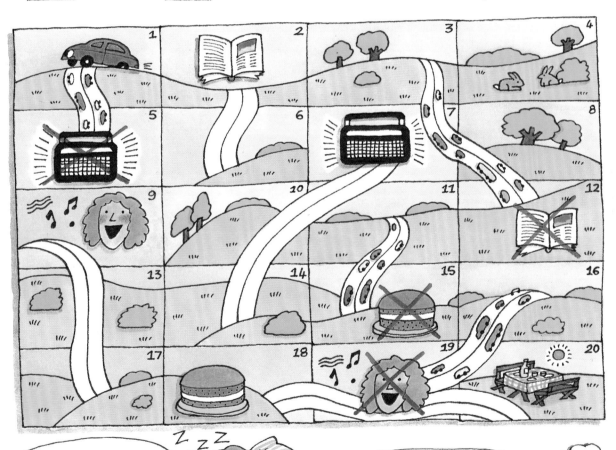

me gusta dormir

me gusta viajar

Can you guess what these two are saying?

Spin a number

You can play this game on your own or with a friend.
Make the spinner from a piece of cardboard. Trace or copy the
shape shown here. Push a pencil or stick through the center.
Twirl the spinner and say the number that it rests on, out loud in
Spanish. Take turns if you are playing with a friend.

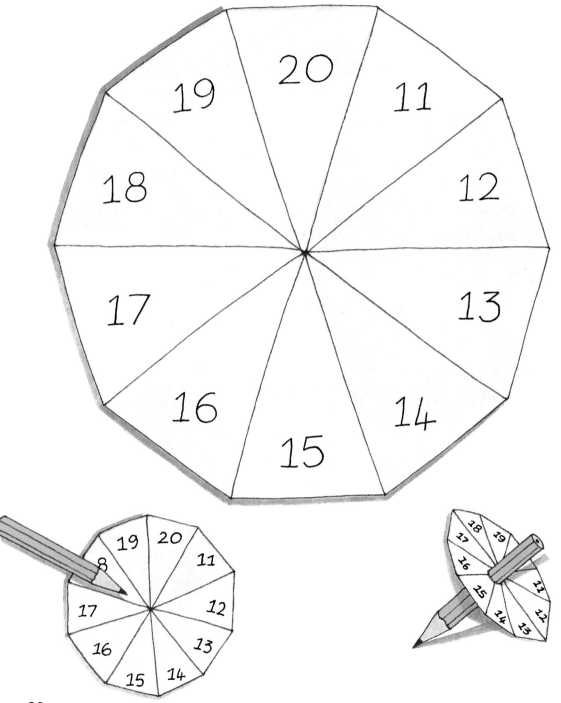

Fun Facts

One of the highest railroads in the world is in Peru and runs from Lima, the capital city, to Huancayo in the Andes mountains. It is so high that they carry special bottles of oxygen on the train to help passengers who suffer from sickness because of the height.

In Spain you can tell what town a car comes from by looking at its license plate, **la matrícula**. For example this car, comes from Madrid. Children have fun on long trips by guessing where the cars come from.

Bingo

Use a pencil to fill in this card with any numbers from 1 to 20. (If you don't press too hard, you can erase them and play again.) Then listen to the tape and cross out the numbers as they are called. Can you get your parents or a friend to play with you and call out different numbers?

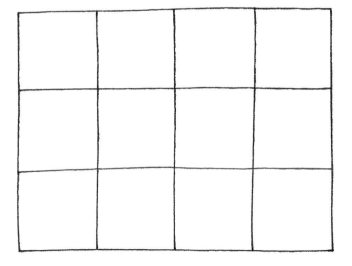

Checklist

Let's go over what you have learned in this unit. When you are sure you know what these mean, put a ✔ in the box.

once doce trece catorce quince

dieciséis diecisiete dieciocho diecinueve veinte

¿qué te gusta hacer?

me gusta cantar
me gusta comer
me gusta escuchar
  la radio

no me gusta viajar
no me gusta leer
no me gusta dormir

Try and say these out loud. If you have any trouble with them, why not listen to the tape again?

¡Super gato!

Me gusta escuchar la radio...

...y me gusta cantar.

¡No me gusta viajar!

40

7 Rojo y negro

In this unit, you're going to learn:

- the colors
- how to say "big" and "small"
- and to understand someone who is asking you what you want.

Listen to the tape before you go on. There's a song to start off with. The words are on page 72.

¿De qué color?

Point to the colors as you hear them on tape.

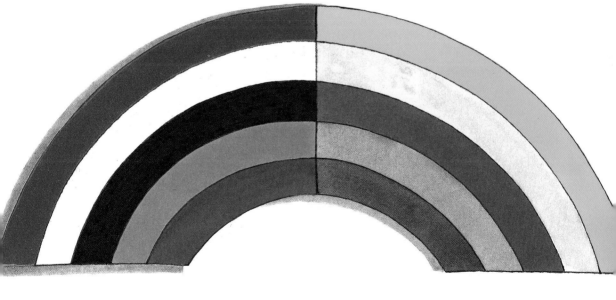

Racing colors

Who will reach the finish line first?
You can play with one or two partners – or even on your own.
Cut out the horses below, and decide who starts. You need a die.

1 *Player 1*: throw the die and move that number of squares along
   the track – counting in Spanish, of course.
2 Each time, say the color of the square you land on in Spanish.
3 If you can't remember it, or if it's wrong, go back two squares.
4 Then it's *Player 2's* turn to throw the die.

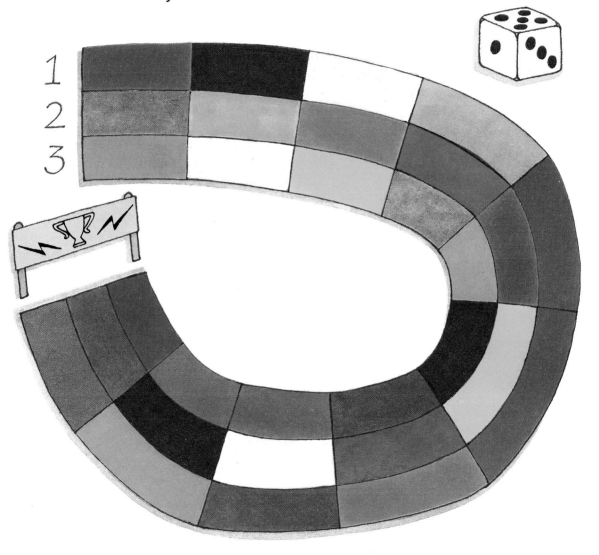

Match the colors

First make 10 cards to match the squares on the boards below, the same size and color. They can be paper or cardboard. Then put them in a box or mix them up on the floor, face down.
You'll need a partner to play this game.
Choose a board and decide who starts.

1 *Player 1:* will pick a card from the box and call out the color in Spanish.
2 Whoever has that color on their board calls out, **"¡es mío!"** (it's mine!).
3 They then take the card and place it on their board on the matching square.
4 Then it's *Player 2's* turn to pick a card.
5 The first to cover a board is the winner.

es mío that's mine/it's mine

Los globos

Listen to the tape.

el globo balloon
¿quieres . . . ? do you want . . . ?
grande big
pequeño small
toma here you are

Take your pick

Listen to the tape. Decide which balloon is being called and mark the correct box.

Fun Facts

Here are three flags of countries where Spanish is spoken. Can you find out what colors they should be and color them in yourself?

México   **España**   **Bolivia**

Checklist

Let's go over what you have learned in this unit. When you are sure you know what these mean, put a ✔ in the box.

☐ **azul rojo negro blanco amarillo**

gris verde morado

marrón naranja

☐ **grande**

☐ **pequeño**

☐ **¿quieres . . . ?**

☐ **toma**

☐ **es mío**

Try and say these out loud. If you have any trouble with them, why not listen to the tape again?

¡Super gato!

En el parque de atracciones.

¡El rojo!

¡El azul!

el parque de atracciones = amusement park

En el bar.

¿Quieres una Coca-Cola también?

en el bar = at the snack bar

BAR

¡Aquí está Monstruorata!

8 El zoo

In this unit, you're going to learn:

- the names of some zoo animals
- how to say you're hungry, thirsty, or afraid
- how to ask for something in a snack bar or restaurant
- how to say that something's super, big, great, etc.

Listen to the tape before you go on.

Los animales

Here are the animals you'll be meeting in this unit. Can you spot 5 differences between the two pictures?

la jirafa

el elefante

el león

el mono

el delfín

Do the activity on page 48 before you go back to the tape.

Giraffe / leaves; dolphin/mouth; elephant/ tusks; monkey/tail; lion/ears.

Where are they?

Fit each animal below into its place in the picture above.

Can you write in the names of these animals in Spanish?

Are they hungry or thirsty?

Listen to the tape.
These animals will say if they are hungry or thirsty.
Draw some food or a drink for them in the box next to each
animal. If you're not sure what they eat, just make it up.

¡Tengo miedo!

¿qué pasa?
what's the matter?
tengo hambre
I'm hungry
tengo sed   I'm thirsty
tengo miedo   I'm scared
yo también   me too

Snick snack

Listen to the children ordering a snack at the zoo snack bar.
Draw a line to connect the food and drink each child orders.
The first one has been done for you.

Now trace or copy those pictures and play a game with a friend.
One person be the snack bar owner and the other ask for a drink and
a snack. Try to use all the language in the hamburger below.
You could also use pictures of other things you already know in
Spanish: ice cream, strawberries, lemonade, and so on.

(un bocadillo), por favor
   (a sandwich), please
eso, por favor that, please
¿algo más? anything else?
¿cuánto es? how much is that?
(doscientas) pesetas (two hundred) pesetas*

*Spanish numbers from 1 to 1000 are on page 68.

Fun Facts

Many of the animals and birds you usually see in zoos come from South America. Right down in the tip of Chile and Argentina, there are seals, **focas**, whales, **ballenas**, and penguins, **pingüinos**.

In the Andes you can see **llamas**, **alpacas,** and **vicuñas**, all part of the camel family. And of course, in the Amazon jungle you can see monkeys, parrots, and the **anaconda** snake, which can grow up to 10 meters, or 30 feet, long. Can you measure that?

¡es grande!   it's big!
¡es bonito!   it's super!
¡es divertido!   it's fun!
¡es estupendo!   it's great!
¡está bueno!   it's good! (of food)

The words for the song are at the back of the book on page 72.

Checklist

Let's go over what you have learned in this unit. When you are sure you know what these mean, put a ✔ in the box.

☐ **¿qué pasa?**

☐ **tengo hambre   tengo sed   tengo miedo**

☐ **el león   el delfín   el mono
el elefante   la jirafa**

☐ **un zumo de naranja   un plátano
un vaso de leche   caramelos
un vaso de agua   un bocadillo**

☐ **¡es grande!   ¡es bonito!   ¡está bueno!
¡es divertido!   ¡es estupendo!**

☐ **eso, por favor   ¿cuánto es?   ¿algo más?**

9 El picnic

In this unit, you're going to learn:
- how to talk about the weather
- how to answer if someone offers you "a little" food
- the names of some food in Spanish.

First let's listen to the weather song on tape. The words are on page 73.

What's the weather like today?

Listen to the tape and write an **✗** next to the right picture.

hace calor it's hot
hace frío it's cold

hace buen tiempo the weather's fine
llueve it's raining

Fun Facts

In Spain, a **tortilla** is an omelette but in Mexico it's a pancake. A **taco** is a Mexican **tortilla** filled with different kinds of fillings, often hot and spicy. You can buy **tacos** on almost every street corner in Mexico and also in a special shop called a **taquería**.

tacos

If you have a picnic in Spain, you will probably take a **tortilla de patata**, a potato omelette – a favorite food. In Colombia, you might take **gallina con papas**, chicken with potatoes; and in Mexico, you might take **tacos** and **enchiladas**, a rolled pancake with a meat or bean filling and hot spices, like chili.

As you can see, potatoes, **patatas**, are popular in Spanish-speaking countries. Did you know that they come from Latin America? They were eaten by Indians in the Andes mountains for over 2000 years before they were taken to Europe.

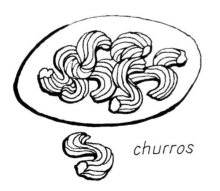

churros

Spanish people do not normally have sweets after their meals. They have fresh fruit for **postre**, dessert, and **pasteles**, cakes, for special occasions. But any time of the day, they can buy sticky doughnuts or fritters called **churros**, from a **churrería** stand or bar.

Turrón is a special candy, like nougat, that Spaniards eat at Christmas time. You have to have strong teeth to bite into it!

Yum, yum

Find the picture that matches the first one in each row.
Check the tape to hear how you say these foods in Spanish.

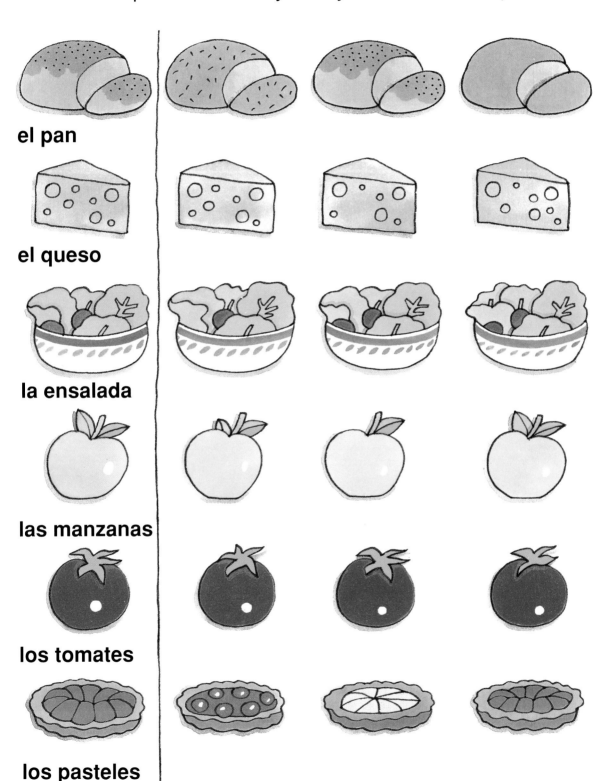

el pan

el queso

la ensalada

las manzanas

los tomates

los pasteles

Al sol

Listen to the conversation on tape.
Here is the picture it's describing.
Can you match the sentences below with the people in the
picture who are saying them?
Write the sentences in the speech bubbles, if you want.

Checklist

Let's go over what you have learned in this unit. When you are sure you know what these mean, put a ✔ in the box.

☐ **hace buen tiempo**

☐ **hace frío**

☐ **hace calor**

☐ **llueve**

☐ **¿quieres un poco de . . . ?**

☐ **el pan**   **la ensalada**
    el queso   **los tomates**
    las manzanas   **los pasteles**

☐ **¡que aproveche!**   **gracias**

Try and say these out loud. If you have any trouble with them, why not listen to the tape again?

¡Super gato!

¡Oh, no! ¡Llueve!

¡Ya está!

ya está = that's it, I'm finished

Hace frío.

In this unit, you're going to learn:

- how to say that you'd like something
- how to say the names of some popular toys
- and you'll go over some of the language you've learned before.

Before you start, listen to the tape. The words for the song are on page 73.

Memory game

Can you remember the names of these things in Spanish?
Say them out loud.
Now listen to the tape again.
Fernando and Susana would like these for their birthday.

Los regalos

Birthday presents. Fit these jigsaw pieces together, and you'll find out what the other children on tape would like for their birthday.

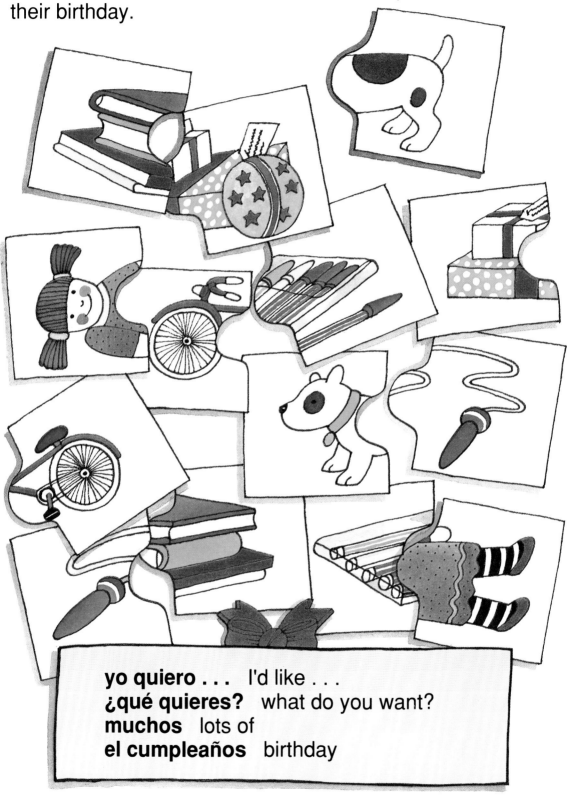

yo quiero . . .   I'd like . . .
¿qué quieres?   what do you want?
muchos   lots of
el cumpleaños   birthday

Pairs game

Make 24 simple cards – two for each of these pictures.

  un gato   **una radio**

 un perro   **unos libros**

caramelos   **unos rotuladores**

 una bicicleta   **una cuerda de saltar**

 un coche   **una muñeca**

un globo  **muchos regalos**

You'll need a partner.
Deal out the cards – 12 each.
The aim is to collect pairs, so lay down any pairs you have at the start.

1 *Player 1:* ask for a card to join to one of yours to make a pair.
   For example, if you have one dog, ask for another.
   Say, **"yo quiero un perro."**
2 Then it's *Player 2's* turn to do the same.
3 The first to lay down all the cards wins.

Fun Facts

When it is your birthday in Spain, you normally get your ear pulled once for every year of your age. This is called **tirones de orejas**. So if you are seven you get your ear pulled seven times. It's supposed to bring you good luck!

In Colombia, birthday girls and boys get eggs thrown at their heads, one for every year!

Party quiz game

It's more fun to play this game with a partner, but you can play on your own too.

You'll need a die and markers.

1. Take turns throwing the die and move your marker along the board.
2. The first to reach the cake wins – but on the way, you must follow the instructions, out loud in Spanish!
3. You miss a turn if you can't answer.

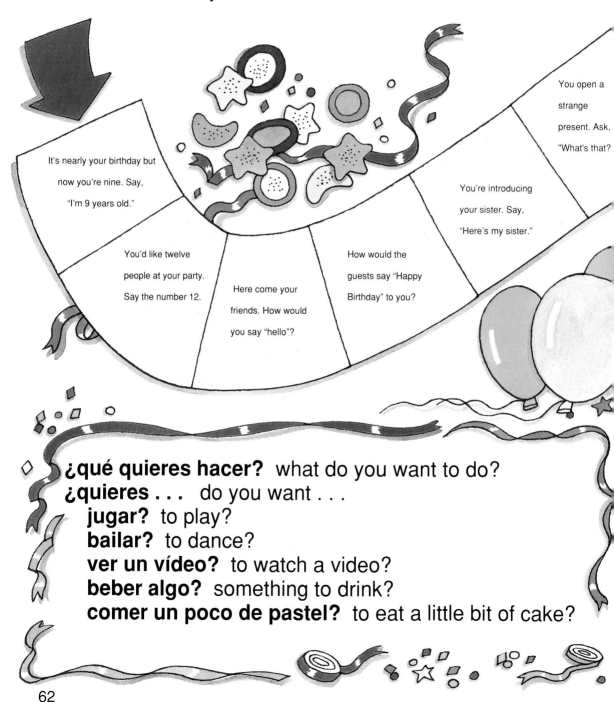

It's nearly your birthday but now you're nine. Say, "I'm 9 years old."

You'd like twelve people at your party. Say the number 12.

Here come your friends. How would you say "hello"?

How would the guests say "Happy Birthday" to you?

You're introducing your sister. Say, "Here's my sister."

You open a strange present. Ask, "What's that?"

¿qué quieres hacer? what do you want to do?
¿quieres . . . do you want . . .
　jugar? to play?
　bailar? to dance?
　ver un vídeo? to watch a video?
　beber algo? something to drink?
　comer un poco de pastel? to eat a little bit of cake?

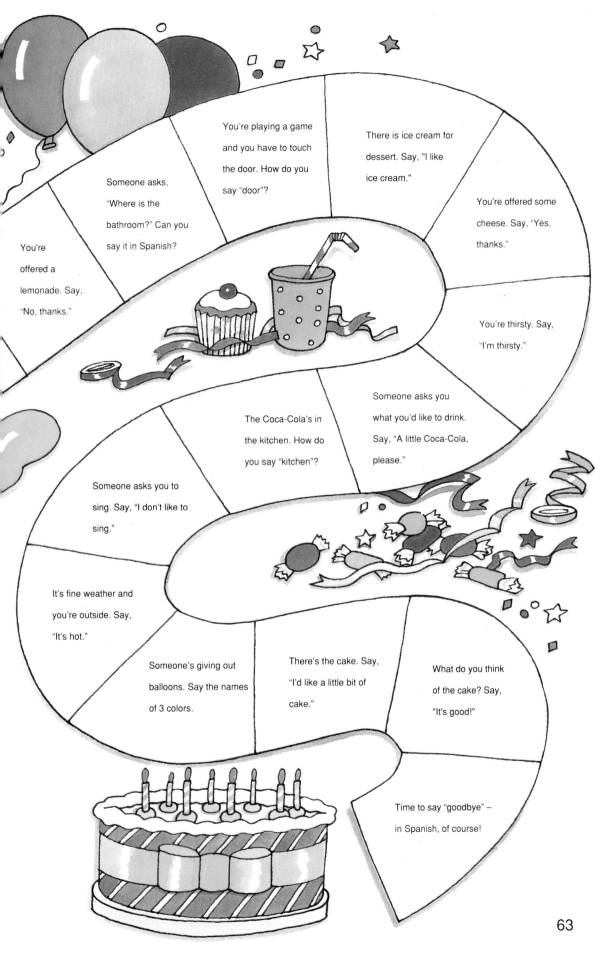

You're playing a game and you have to touch the door. How do you say "door"?

There is ice cream for dessert. Say, "I like ice cream."

Someone asks, "Where is the bathroom?" Can you say it in Spanish?

You're offered some cheese. Say, "Yes, thanks."

You're offered a lemonade. Say, "No, thanks."

You're thirsty. Say, "I'm thirsty."

The Coca-Cola's in the kitchen. How do you say "kitchen"?

Someone asks you what you'd like to drink. Say, "A little Coca-Cola, please."

Someone asks you to sing. Say, "I don't like to sing."

It's fine weather and you're outside. Say, "It's hot."

Someone's giving out balloons. Say the names of 3 colors.

There's the cake. Say, "I'd like a little bit of cake."

What do you think of the cake? Say, "It's good!"

Time to say "goodbye" – in Spanish, of course!

63

Checklist

Let's go over what you have learned in this unit. When you are sure you know what these mean, put a ✔ in the box.

☐ **¿qué quieres?**

☐ **yo quiero . . .**

☐ **un perro   una cuerda de saltar**
un pastel   una muñeca   unos rotuladores
unos libros   una bicicleta   muchos regalos

☐ **¿qué quieres hacer?**

☐ **¿quieres ... ?**
bailar?   ver un vídeo?
jugar?   beber algo?

☐ **¡feliz cumpleaños!**

More about Spanish

Learning a language is like breaking a code or recognizing patterns. Did you notice some patterns in the Spanish you have just learned? Have a look at these:

The words for "the"

There are four words for "the" in Spanish:

• **el** and **la**

el gato   the cat
la casa   the house

• and **los** and **las** when there is more than one thing:

los gatos   the cats
las casas   the houses

The words for "a"

There are two words for "a" in Spanish:

• **un** and **una**

un gato   a cat
una casa   a house

Can you spot the pattern?
If you use **el** for "the," you use **un** for "a."
And if you use **la** for "the," you use **una** for "a."

The **el/un** words are called *masculine*.
The **la/una** words are called *feminine*.
All *nouns* (objects, people, and places) in Spanish are either masculine or feminine.

As you would expect, the words for "man" and "boy" are masculine, and the words for "woman" and "girl" are feminine.
Look at these examples:

un hombre	a man	**una mujer**	a woman
un chico	a boy	**una chica**	a girl
un padre	a father	**una madre**	a mother
un tío	an uncle	**una tía**	an aunt
un profesor	a man teacher	**una profesora**	a woman teacher

Most nouns that finish in **-o** are masculine and most nouns that finish in **-a** are feminine. But for a lot of nouns, there's no easy way of telling whether you should use **el** or **la** or **un** or **una** – you just have to learn each word! Don't panic, after a while you can *hear* if you've got it right . . . and people will still understand you even if you get it wrong.

More than one thing

Look at this pattern:

casa   house
casas   houses

gato   cat
gatos   cats

profesor   man teacher
profesores   men teachers

pastel   cake
pasteles   cakes

So, in Spanish, in the plural (when you have more than one of something):
• you add an **-s**, like **casas** and **gatos**
• or you add **-es**, like **profesores** and **pasteles**.

Try to say those words out loud. If you can't remember how to pronounce them, listen to your cassettes again.

No, not

You know how to say:

me gusta bailar   I like to dance
no me gusta bailar   I don't like to dance

And look at:

tengo sed   I'm thirsty
no tengo sed   I'm not thirsty

Can you see the pattern?
In Spanish, to change to the *negative* (saying "no" or "not"), you use **no**.

Look at these:

me gusta el helado   I like ice cream
tengo una hermana   I have a sister
hace calor   it's hot
tengo hambre   I'm hungry

How would you say these in Spanish?

I do *not* like ice cream
I do *not* have a sister
it's *not* hot
I'm *not* hungry

The answers are upside down at the foot of the page.

As you get better at Spanish, keep trying to break the code and discover more patterns. Soon you'll be able to make up your own sentences.
(There are lots of patterns to discover in the numbers on the next page!)

Answers

no me gusta el helado
no tengo una hermana
no hace calor
no tengo hambre

Numbers 1 to 1000

The numbers in parentheses are used with *feminine* nouns, like **casa**, house, or **hermana**, sister. (See *More about Spanish* on page 65.)

1	uno (una)		50	cincuenta
2	dos		51	cincuenta y uno (una)
3	tres		52	cincuenta y dos
4	cuatro			
5	cinco		and then the same pattern to . . . 59	
6	seis		60	sesenta
7	siete		61	sesenta y uno (una)
8	ocho		62	sesenta y dos
9	nueve			
10	diez		and then the same pattern to . . . 69	

1	uno (una)
2	dos
3	tres
4	cuatro
5	cinco
6	seis
7	siete
8	ocho
9	nueve
10	diez
11	once
12	doce
13	trece
14	catorce
15	quince
16	dieciséis
17	diecisiete
18	dieciocho
19	diecinueve
20	veinte
21	veintiuno (-una)
22	veintidós
23	veintitrés
24	veinticuatro
25	veinticinco
26	veintiséis
27	veintisiete
28	veintiocho
29	veintinueve
30	treinta
31	treinta y uno (una)
32	treinta y dos

continue the pattern to . . . 39

40	cuarenta
41	cuarenta y uno (una)
42	cuarenta y dos

and on with the same pattern to . . . 49

50	cincuenta
51	cincuenta y uno (una)
52	cincuenta y dos

and then the same pattern to . . . 59

60	sesenta
61	sesenta y uno (una)
62	sesenta y dos

and then the same pattern to . . . 69

70	setenta
71	setenta y uno (una)
72	setenta y dos

and the same pattern to . . . 79

80	ochenta
81	ochenta y uno (una)
82	ochenta y dos

now follow the usual pattern to . . . 89

90	noventa
91	noventa y uno (una)
92	noventa y dos

and the same pattern to . . . 99

100	cien
101	ciento uno (una)
102	ciento dos

and the same pattern as from 1 to 100 up to . . . 199

200	doscientos (-as)
300	trescientos (-as)
400	cuatrocientos (-as)
500	quinientos (-as)
600	seiscientos (-as)
700	setecientos (-as)
800	ochocientos (-as)
900	novecientos (-as)
1000	mil

Songs

Unit 1

Hola, me llamo Miguel.
¿Cómo te llamas?
Hola, me llamo Miguel.
¿Cómo te llamas?

Hola, me llamo Miguel.
¿Cómo te llamas?
Hola, me llamo Miguel.
¿Cómo te llamas?

Me llamo Miguel.
¡Hola!

Hola, me llamo Raquel.
¿Cómo te llamas?
Hola, me llamo Raquel.
¿Cómo te llamas?

Hola, me llamo Raquel.
¿Cómo te llamas?
Hola, me llamo Raquel.
¿Cómo te llamas?

Me llamo Raquel.
¡Hola!

¡Hola!

Uno, dos, tres,
Cuatro, cinco, seis,
Siete, ocho, nueve,
Diez.

Uno, dos, tres,
Cuatro, cinco, seis,
Siete, ocho, nueve,
Diez.

Unit 2

¿Te gusta la Coca-Cola?
No.
¿Te gusta la gaseosa?
No.
¿Te gusta el helado?
No.
¿Te gustan las pizzas?
Sí.
Sólo las pizzas.
Sólo las pizzas.

¿Te gustan las fresas?
No.
¿Te gustan los gatos?
No.
¿Te gusta el helado?
No.
¿Te gustan las pizzas?
Sí.
Sólo las pizzas.
Sólo las pizzas.

sólo = only

Unit 3

Me gusta el colegio.
Me gusta el colegio.
Uno, dos, tres.
Cuatro, cinco, seis.
Me gusta el colegio.
Me gusta el colegio.
Siete, ocho, nueve,
Diez.

Me gusta el colegio.
Me gusta el colegio.
Uno, dos, tres.
Cuatro, cinco, seis.
Me gusta el colegio.
Me gusta el colegio.
Siete, ocho, nueve,
Diez.

¿Dónde está la clase?
¿Dónde está el patio?
¿Dónde está la clase?
¿Dónde está el patio?

Me gusta el colegio.
Me gusta el colegio.
Uno, dos, tres.
Cuatro, cinco, seis.
Me gusta el colegio.
Me gusta el colegio.
Siete, ocho, nueve,
Diez.

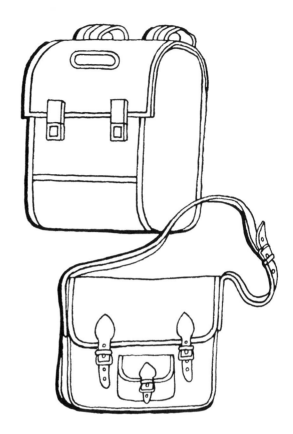

Unit 4

Ésta es mi familia.
Ésta es mi familia.
Ésta es mi mamá,
Éste es mi papá.
Ésta es mi familia.
Ésta es mi familia.
Tengo dos hermanos
Y tengo tres hermanas.

Ésta es mi familia.
Ésta es mi familia.
Ésta es abuelita,
Éste es abuelito.
Ésta es mi familia.
Ésta es mi familia.
Tengo dos hermanos
Y tengo tres hermanas.

Unit 5

¿Qué es esto?
¿Qué es esto?
Es una bruja.
¿Qué es esto?
¿Qué es esto?
Es una bruja.

¿Dónde está la bruja?
Está aquí.
¿Dónde está la bruja?
En la cocina.
¿Dónde está la bruja?
Está aquí.
¡Hola! ¡Hola!

¿Qué es esto?
¿Qué es esto?
Es una bruja.
¿Qué es esto?
¿Qué es esto?
Es una bruja.

¿Qué es esto?
¿Qué es esto?
Es una bruja.
¿Qué es esto?
¿Qué es esto?
Es una bruja.

en = in

Unit 6

No me gusta comer.
No me gusta beber.
No me gusta leer.
¡Me gusta dormir!

No me gusta viajar.
No me gusta jugar.
No me gusta cantar.
¡Me gusta dormir!

¿Te gusta escuchar
La radio?
¡No me gusta escuchar
La radio, no!

No me gusta comer.
No me gusta beber.
No me gusta leer.
¡Me gusta dormir!

beber = to drink
jugar = to play

Unit 7

Negro,
Blanco,
Rojo, amarillo, azul.
Negro,
Blanco,
Rojo, amarillo, azul.

Rojo y azul dan morado.
Azul y amarillo dan verde.
Amarillo y rojo dan naranja.
Me gusta naranja.
Me gusta naranja.

Negro,
Blanco,
Rojo, amarillo, azul.
Negro,
Blanco,
Rojo, amarillo, azul.

dan = make

Unit 8

Vamos al zoo,
Vamos al zoo,
A ver los animales,
Vamos al zoo.

Vamos al zoo,
Vamos al zoo,
A ver los animales,
Vamos al zoo.

Camellos, leones, monos,
jirafas.
Camellos, leones, monos,
jirafas.
Delfines y elefantes,
Uno, dos, tres elefantes.

Vamos al zoo,
Vamos al zoo,
A ver los animales,
Vamos al zoo.

vamos = let's go
a ver = to see
camellos = camels

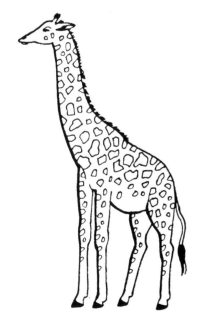

Unit 9

Hace buen tiempo.
Hoy hace calor.
Un picnic, muy bien, vamos.
Hace buen tiempo.
Hoy hace calor.
Un picnic, muy bien, vamos.

Hace buen tiempo.
Hoy hace calor.
Un picnic, muy bien, vamos.
Hace buen tiempo.
Hoy hace calor.
Un picnic, muy bien, vamos.

¡Oh no, oh no!
Ahora llueve, sí.
¡Oh no, oh no!
Y hace frío
Aquí.

Hace buen tiempo.
Hoy hace calor.
Un picnic, muy bien, vamos.
Hace buen tiempo.
Hoy hace calor.
Un picnic, muy bien, vamos.

Hace buen tiempo.
Hoy hace calor.
Un picnic, muy bien, vamos.
Hace buen tiempo.
Hoy hace calor.
Un picnic, muy bien, vamos.

hoy = today
muy bien = very good
vamos = let's go
ahora = now
y = and

Unit 10

Es tu cumpleaños.
Es tu cumpleaños.
¿Quieres jugar?
¿Quieres bailar?
Es tu cumpleaños.
Es tu cumpleaños.
¿Quieres comer?
¿Qué quieres hacer?

Toma un regalo.
Es un perrito.
Toma un regalo.
Se llama Pepito.

Es tu cumpleaños.
Es tu cumpleaños.
¿Quieres jugar?
¿Quieres bailar?
Es tu cumpleaños.
Es tu cumpleaños.
¿Quieres comer?
¿Qué quieres hacer?
¿Quieres comer?
¿Qué quieres hacer?

tu = your
toma = here is
perrito = little dog
se llama = it's called

Word list

All the Spanish nouns are listed with **el** or **la**.

Spanish–English

A

a to;
  al (zoo) to the (zoo)
la abuelita grandma
el abuelito grandpa
los abuelos
  grandparents
adiós goodbye
el agua water
ahora now
algo something;
  ¿algo más? anything
  else?
allí there
amarillo yellow
los amigos friends
el animal animal
el año year;
  **¿cuántos años
  tienes?** how old are
  you?;
  tengo . . . años
  I'm . . . (years old)
aquí here;
  está aquí it's here
la araña spider
azul blue

B

bailar to dance
la ballena whale
el banco bank

el bar snack bar
beber to drink
la bicicleta bike
bien good, well, fine,
  OK
blanco white
el bocadillo sandwich
¡bonito! super!
¡bravo! good! well
  done!
la bruja witch
¡buena suerte! good
  luck!
buen, bueno, buena
  good;
  está bueno it's good
  (for food);
  buenos días good
  day
el bumerán boomerang

C

el calor heat;
  hace calor *(weather)*
  it's hot
la cama bed
el camello camel
el canguro kangaroo
cantar to sing
el caramelo candy
la casa house
catorce fourteen
cinco five

la clase class
la Coca-Cola Coca-Cola
el coche car
la cocina kitchen
el colegio school
el color color;
  ¿de qué color (es)?
  what color (is it)?;
  de todos los colores
  of all colors
comer to eat
¿cómo te llamas?
  what's your name?
contar to count
¿cuándo? when?
¿cuánto? how much?;
  ¿cuánto es? how
  much is that?;
  **¿cuántos años
  tienes?** how old are
  you?
el cuarto de baño
  bathroom
cuatro four
la cuerda de saltar
  jump rope
el cumpleaños
  birthday;
  ¡feliz cumpleaños!
  happy birthday!

CH

la chica girl

el chico boy
el chocolate chocolate

D

dan they give
de of, from, on
el delfín dolphin
el día day;
  buenos días good day
diecinueve nineteen
dieciocho eighteen
dieciséis sixteen
diecisiete seventeen
diez ten
divertido fun
doce twelve
¿dónde? where?;
  ¿dónde está? where is?;
  ¿dónde están? where are?
dormir to sleep
el dormitorio bedroom *(Spain)*
dos two

E

el the
el elefante elephant
en in, at, on
la ensalada salad
es is, it is
la escuela primaria elementary school
¡escucha! listen!
eso that;
  ¡eso es! that's right!
ésta/éste/esto this

está is
están are
¡estupendo! great!

F

la familia family
feliz happy;
  ¡feliz cumpleaños! happy birthday!
la fresa strawberry
el frío cold;
  hace frío *(weather)* it's cold
el frigorífico fridge

G

la gaseosa soda pop; lemonade
el gato cat
el globo balloon
gordo fat
gracias thanks, thank you
grande big
gris gray
gusta, gustan like;
  me gusta *(one thing)* I like
  me gustan *(many things)* I like
  ¿te gusta? *(one thing)* do you like?;
  ¿te gustan? *(many things)* do you like?

H

hacer to do;
  hace buen tiempo the weather's fine

hambre: tengo hambre I'm hungry
hasta until;
  hasta luego see you later/soon;
  hasta mañana see you tomorrow
el helado ice cream
la hermana sister
el hermano brother
el hombre man
¡hola! hello!; hi!
hoy today

I

el inspector inspector

J

la jirafa giraffe
jugar to play
el jugo fruit juice *(Latin America)*
el jugo de naranja orange juice
juntos together

L

la the
el ladrón thief
las the
el lavabo sink
la leche milk
leer to read
el león lion
el libro book
los the

LL

llamar to call;
  ¿cómo te llamas?
  what's your name?;
  me llamo . . . my
  name is . . .;
  se llama it's called
llueve it's raining

M

la madre mother
la mamá Mom
la manzana apple
más more
marrón brown
me myself
la mesa table
mi my
mí me
miedo: tengo miedo
  I'm scared
mío mine;
  es mío it's mine
el mono monkey
el monstruo monster
morado purple
mucho a lot;
  muchos regalos lots
  of presents
la mujer woman
la muñeca doll
muy very;
  ¡muy bien! very
  good!; very well!

N

la naranja *(fruit)* orange
naranja *(color)* orange

negro black
no no, not
nueve nine

O

o or
ocho eight
once eleven
el oro gold

P

el padre father
el pan bread
el papá dad
para for
¡para! stop!
el parque de
  atracciones
  amusement park
el pastel cake, tart
la pastelería bakery
el patio playground
pequeño small
el perro dog
la peseta peseta
  (Spanish money)
el peso peso *(money of*
  some Latin American
  countries)
el picnic picnic
la piedra pebble
la pizza pizza
el plátano banana
poco little;
  un poco de queso a
  little bit of cheese
por favor please
preparados ready

el profesor *(man)*
  teacher
la profesora *(woman)*
  teacher
la puerta door

Q

¿qué? what?;
  ¿qué es esto? what's
  this?;
  ¿qué pasa? what's
  the matter?;
  ¿qué tal? how are
  things?
¡que aproveche! enjoy
  your meal!
el queso cheese
¿quieres? do you
  want?
quiero I'd like; I want
quince fifteen

R

la radio radio
la recámara bedroom
  (Mexico)
el regalo present
rojo red
el rotulador felt-tip pen

S

el saco bag
saltar to jump;
  una cuerda de saltar
  jump rope
el salón living room
sed: tengo sed I'm
  thirsty

seis six
señor Mr.
señora Mrs.
el servicio public bathroom
sí yes
siete seven
la silla chair
el sol sun;
　al sol in the sun
sólo only
soy I am
suerte luck;
　¡buena suerte! good luck!

T

el taco meat-filled pancake *(Mexico)*
también also;
　yo también me too!
te you, yourself;
　te toca a ti your turn
la tele television
(yo) tengo I have
el tiempo weather;
　hace buen tiempo the weather is fine
(tu) tienes you have
la tía aunt
el tío uncle
toma here is; here you are
el tomate tomato
la tortilla omelette *(Spain)*; pancake *(Mexico)*
trece thirteen
tres three

tú you
tu your

U

un, **una** a
una, **uno** one
unos some

V

¡vamos! let's go!; go ahead!
¡vamos a . . . ! let's . . . !
el vaso glass
veinte twenty
ver to see, to watch
verde green
viajar to travel
el viaje trip
el vídeo video, videocassette

Y

y and
ya already;
　ya está that's it, I'm finished
yo I, me;
　yo quiero I'd like . . .;
　yo también me too

Z

el zoo zoo
el zumo fruit juice *(Spain)*;
　el zumo de naranja orange juice

English–Spanish

A

a un, una
also también
amusement park el parque de atracciones
and y
animal el animal
anything algo;
　anything else? ¿algo más?
apple la manzana
at en
aunt la tía

B

bag el saco
bakery la pastelería
balloon el globo
banana el plátano
bank el banco
bathroom el cuarto de baño; *(public)* el servicio
bed la cama
bedroom *(Spain)* el dormitorio; *(Mexico)* la recámara
big grande
bike la bicicleta
birthday el cumpleaños;
　happy birthday! ¡feliz cumpleaños!
black negro
blue azul
book el libro

boomerang el bumerán
boy el chico
bread el pan
brother el hermano
brown marrón

C

cake el pastel
called: it's called se llama
camel el camello
candy el caramelo
car el coche
cat el gato
chair la silla
cheese el queso
chocolate el chocolate
class la clase
Coca-Cola la Coca-Cola
cold el frío;
  it's cold *(weather)* hace frío
color el color
  what color (is it)? ¿de qué color (es)?;
  of all colors de todos los colores
to count contar

D

dad el papá
to dance bailar
day el día
to do hacer;
  what do you like to do? ¿qué te gusta hacer?
dog el perro

doll la muñeca
dolphin el delfín
door la puerta
to drink beber

E

to eat comer
eight ocho
eighteen dieciocho
elephant el elefante
eleven once
enjoy your meal! ¡que aproveche!

F

family la familia
fat gordo
father el padre
felt-tip pen el rotulador
fifteen quince
fine bien
five cinco
for de, para, por
four cuatro
fourteen catorce
fridge el frigorífico
friends los amigos
from de
fruit juice *(Mexico)* el jugo; *(Spain)* el zumo
fun divertido

G

giraffe la jirafa
girl la chica
glass el vaso
go: let's go!; go ahead! ¡vamos!
gold el oro

good bien, bueno, buena; *(well done!)* ¡bravo!;
  good day buenos días;
  good luck! ¡buena suerte!;
  it's good *(for food)* está bueno
goodbye adiós
grandma la abuelita
grandpa el abuelito
grandparents los abuelos
gray gris
great! ¡estupendo!
green verde

H

happen: what's happening ¿qué pasa?
happy feliz;
  happy birthday! ¡feliz cumpleaños!
(I) have (yo) tengo
(you) have (tú) tienes
heat el calor;
  it's hot *(weather)* hace calor
hello! ¡hola!
here aquí
  it's here está aquí
  here is, **here you are** toma
hi! ¡hola!
house la casa
how are you? ¿qué tal?

how much ¿cuánto?;
  how much is that?
  ¿cuánto es?
how old are you?
  ¿cuántos años tienes?
hungry: I'm hungry
  tengo hambre

I

I am soy
I yo;
  I'd like . . . yo quiero
ice cream el helado
in en
inspector el inspector
is, it is es; está;
  it's OK está bien

J

jump rope la cuerda de
  saltar

K

kangaroo el canguro
kitchen la cocina

L

lemonade la gaseosa
let's go! ¡vamos!;
  let's . . . ! ¡vamos a . . . !
like gusta, gustan;
  I like (one thing) me
  gusta
  I like (many things)
  me gustan
  do you like (one thing)
  ¿te gusta?;
  do you like (many
  things) ¿te gustan?

lion el león
to listen escuchar;
  listen! ¡escucha!
little poco;
  a little bit of cheese
  un poco de queso
living room el salón
lot mucho
luck suerte;
  good luck! ¡buena
  suerte!

M

man el hombre
me mí;
  me too! yo también
milk la leche
mine mío;
  it's mine es mío
Mom la mamá
monkey el mono
monster el monstruo
morning la mañana
more más
Mr. señor
Mrs. señora
my mi
myself me

N

nine nueve
nineteen diecinueve
no, **not** no
now ahora

O

of de
on de, en
one uno, una

only sólo
or o
orange (fruit) la
  naranja; (color) naranja
orange juice el zumo
  de naranja (Spain); el
  jugo de naranja
  (Mexico)

P

pebble la piedra
picnic el picnic
pizza la pizza
to play jugar
playground el patio
please por favor
present el regalo
purple morado

R

radio la radio
it's raining llueve
to read leer
ready preparados
red rojo

S

salad la ensalada
sandwich el bocadillo
scared: I'm scared
  tengo miedo
school el colegio;
  elementary school la
  escuela primaria
to see ver
see you later, **see you
  soon** hasta luego
see you tomorrow
  hasta mañana

seven siete
seventeen diecisiete
to sing cantar
sink el lavabo
sister la hermana
six seis
sixteen dieciséis
to sleep dormir
small pequeño
snack bar el bar
soda pop la gaseosa
some unos, unas
spider la araña
stop! ¡para!
strawberry la fresa
sun el sol;
  in the sun al sol
super bonito
sweet el caramelo

T

table la mesa
teacher *(man)* el profesor; *(woman)* la profesora
television la tele
ten diez
thank you gracias
that eso;
  that's right! ¡eso es!
the el, la, los, las
there allí
thief el ladrón
thirsty: I'm thirsty tengo sed
thirteen trece
this ésta, éste, esto
three tres

to a
today hoy
together juntos
tomato el tomate
tomorrow mañana
too también
to travel viajar
trip el viaje
twelve doce
twenty veinte
two dos

U

uncle el tío
until hasta

V

very muy;
  very good!, very well! ¡muy bien!
videocassette el vídeo

W

to want querer;
  do you want? ¿quieres?;
  I want quiero;
  what do you want? ¿qué quieres?
to watch ver
water el agua
weather: the weather is fine hace buen tiempo
whale la ballena
what? ¿qué?;
  what do you like to do? ¿qué te gusta hacer?;

what do you want to do? ¿qué quieres hacer?;
what's the matter? ¿qué pasa?;
what's this? ¿qué es esto?;
what's your name? ¿cómo te llamas?
when? ¿cuándo?
where? ¿dónde?
white blanco
witch la bruja
woman la mujer

Y

yellow amarillo
yes sí
you te, tú
your tu
yourself te
your turn te toca a ti

Z

zoo el zoo